GIRAFFE'S Tale

Margaret D. Finlay

This book is dedicated to the memory of David.

Margaret D. Findlay is married and has three children. Her second child, David, died. Because of health problems two of Margaret's children were perceived as 'different'. It was from this that the idea for 'Giraffe's Tale' derived. Margaret is a wonderfully warm Christian and an active member of Struther's Memorial Church, Edinburgh. She is a housewife, a play group leader and a children's storyteller.

Cover illustration by Lee Gallaher
Book illustration by Glynn Marshall

First published 1995

Published by Autumn House
Alma Park, Grantham, NG31 9SL, England.

ISBN 1-873796-46-3

Three pairs of bright eyes peeped out of the thick bushes.

'That's it. Over there!' whispered Ben, the largest of the young badgers.

'Ooh! How strange!' squeaked a small voice.

'Ssh! It will hear us, Billy,' said Brenda, placing a paw firmly over her young brother's mouth.

In the clearing, quietly munching a mouthful of fresh green leaves, was a giraffe.

Jeremy, the giraffe, had arrived in Chestnut Wood one spring day. He had run away from his owner! Although he had many friends where he lived, the owner had been cruel to him. One night he had noticed the gate to his small field was unlocked. He decided to escape across the fields and find a new home.

DO NOT
CROSS

Many of the animals in Chestnut Village had seen him walking in their wood and were very frightened. No one had ever seen a giraffe before.

'He'll eat us all!' they cried.

'He'll trample on us. He won't be able to see us, we're so small!' said others. Many even called him ugly.

It was decided, in the end, that the bravest, strongest animals in Chestnut Village would go down to the river bank. From there they would shout a warning to the giraffe to tell him he was not wanted there, and that he must *never* cross the river.

Four foxes were chosen for the job.

'Do not cross the river *EVER!*' they shouted together.

Jeremy the giraffe did not have a chance to argue. The foxes darted away as soon as they finished shouting.

They returned to the village and proudly told the villagers how they had scared the creature away. They added that there would be no more trouble from him.

A little mouse listened to the villagers and felt sad. 'What trouble has he caused? How do they *know* he will trample on them?' she asked herself.

Jeremy didn't want to go where he wasn't wanted, so he started to search for a home on his side of the river. At the edge of the wood there was an old ruined castle. Some of its walls had tumbled down but it did have one good room. Jeremy knew he could make it comfortable. The garden was full of tasty leaves and the castle was not far from the river. Everything seemed perfect, but the friendly giraffe was sad and lonely.

Sometimes he could hear scratching and rustlings among the bushes. One day he saw three pairs of eyes watching him. But Jeremy knew that if he took one step towards the animals they would run away.

Often Jeremy thought he should move away to another wood, but he was afraid to go out into the open field in case his cruel owner saw him.

And now there was another reason for not wanting to go — he had made a friend at last.

Each morning Jeremy went down to the river to drink. From the river bank he would look across to Chestnut Village School. One morning he saw a tiny white thing waving. It was a hanky belonging to a small mouse. She was jumping up and down and smiling at him.

From that moment on, the best part of the giraffe's day was when he went down to the river and waved a leafy branch to his new friend.

The three young badgers, like all the school animals, were curious about the strange creature their parents had warned them about. That was why, early one morning, they went to find out if it was as terrible as they had been told. Now they would be late for school if they were not quick.

'He wasn't *that* horrible,' said Brenda. '*I* don't think he looked fierce.'

'What would *you* know?' said her big brother. 'Animals that big *are* dangerous!'

'Quick, it's the bell! We'll be late!' cried Brenda, grabbing young Billy's paw. 'Hurry up!'

As they ran into school, Brenda wondered about the strange creature, and the little mouse who was her best friend. She had often seen her waving her hanky and smiling to him. He always smiled back and seemed pleased to see the mouse. He was not at all fierce.

Brenda's big brother ran into school feeling very excited. He could not wait to tell his friends how brave he had been. He had faced the enemy! He had shown the huge creature with the long neck who was boss!

William
BRENDA
Ben

Jeremy was sad as he watched the three badgers scurry away. No one ever talked to him. They did not want to hear his story, or be his friends. Then he remembered the little mouse and smiled to himself. She was the smallest animal he had ever seen — but she had the biggest smile and her little black eyes were very kind.

As the badgers scurried off to school, they didn't know that someone else had been watching *them* watching the giraffe. It was a weasel!

The weasels lived in the wood on Jeremy's side of the river. The village animals often talked about them, but

none of them ever went into the woods to see them. Seven weasels lived in the wood. They were wild, cruel creatures who frightened the villagers.

PC Hedgehog often had to help animals whose houses had been robbed. Weasel footprints were found near the houses, but no one could catch the thieves.

Poor Squirrel, who owned the village shop, was very frightened of the weasels. With scarfs over their faces they would go into his shop and steal food.

Now the weasels had a wicked *new* plan. The biggest and wickedest plan ever. But first they must make the villagers hate the giraffe even more.

In Chestnut Village's Town Hall was a wonderful collection of silver. There were valuable old cups and plates from the ruined castle where Jeremy lived. And there were beautiful candlesticks from the old church. Many silver trophies won by the village animals were on show. There were medals for bravery. The plates for 'Best-kept Village' were there too.

The weasels planned to steal them all!

One dark night the seven sly creatures gathered in the wood. As smoke from their camp fire curled up into the cold air, all whispering died away as the leader began to speak.

'Right, boys! I want that silver and I want it soon! Do you all know what you have to do?'

One by one, weasel voices answered. 'Yeah! We're going to visit the village, all peaceable-like, and tell them that giraffe's a thief!' Sniggers were heard as another said, 'Then when things go missing they will know where to look!'

'Yeah!' snarled one weasel. '*We* shall have the silver, and that stupid giraffe will get the blame!'

There was a lot of wicked laughter until the leader shouted for silence.

'Here's the plan. We'll start some trouble in the village. While those silly animals are dealing with it, we'll steal all the silver from the Town Hall and get back here double quick.'

Suddenly the leader pointed to a one-eyed weasel. 'You will take one silver cup, a small one, mind, and hide it in the giraffe's home. That will make everyone believe that the giraffe is the thief. It will be easy, because they hate him anyway.'

Cheering and laughter filled the air as the weasels settled down to an evening of eating, drinking, and story-telling.

One morning, after breakfast, Jeremy went to the river for a drink. He knew he was too early to see the little mouse. She came to wave at playtime. But he looked for her anyway.

While waiting for the little mouse to appear, Jeremy sat and watched the village. He saw the animals coming and going about their daily work. He tried to imagine where they lived. He even made up names for them. He wondered if he would ever be asked to cross the river and join them.

Suddenly Jeremy forgot his day-dream as he noticed some scruffy-looking weasels leave the woods. They crossed the river on the old log-crossing instead of by the bridge, and went into the village. They looked about them in a sneaky manner, and Jeremy knew they were up to no good.

And sure enough, he saw them steal apples, oranges and pears from a fruit stall. With bulging pockets they moved on through the village.

Jeremy noticed how the villagers smiled and nodded to them as they hurried past. He also saw one of the gang take a hedgehog's purse from her baby's pram when she wasn't looking. And he wondered why these creatures were allowed in the village when he was not. He would never have hurt anyone or taken things which did not belong to him.

Now Jeremy saw that two of the weasels had reached the school. Then suddenly they disappeared.

'How strange,' thought Jeremy. 'Oh! there you are!' he said to himself as one of the weasels slipped down into the school's boiler room through the coal door. 'So, it's coal you're after.'

But a movement by the Town Hall caught his eye. He was just in time to see one of the other weasels squeeze in through a tiny side window. Everyone had gone to lunch, so the doors were locked.

'Now what do they want in the Town Hall?' Jeremy wondered. 'There's nothing in there for them.'

But something happened that made Jeremy forget the weasels and the Town Hall. Out of the corner of his eye he saw that smoke was billowing out of the doors and windows of the school. In the playground badgers, foxes, hedgehogs and squirrels were running around in all directions. Jeremy watched as they joined up to make a line to the river, and started to pass buckets of water up to the school.

One by one the animals threw the water on the flames. But it was no good. The fire was out of control. Even across the river Jeremy could smell the burning wood. He could hear the cries of the frightened animals.

'It's not working!' He said to himself. 'If only I could help.'

'Do not cross the river *EVER!*' He remembered the foxes' words.

Suddenly an upstairs window was flung open, and Jeremy saw his little friend the mouse leaning out, waving her handkerchief. But this time it was in fright. She was not looking down at the anxious parents in the playground, but out across the river towards Jeremy!

'Oh, what can I do?' he moaned. Then he decided. 'They can do what they like to me, but I've got to help my little *friend*.'

In a few strides his long legs took him over the river and into the playground. He was greeted by screams and growls and some of the animals hit his legs with sticks. Jeremy ignored them and ran to the window to save the little mouse.

'Little mouse! Slide down my neck and be quick! Get your friends to do the same.'

No one hit Jeremy now. All eyes were on him as frightened and sooty creatures climbed out of the window and slid down his long neck.

'Amazing!' cried a mother hedgehog.

'It's wonderful. They'll all be saved!' shouted a father fox. But the smile faded from his face as he remembered how he had shouted cruelly at the giraffe not so long ago.

FIRE 1

Through the thick smoke Jeremy shouted, 'The weasels did this! They're in the Town Hall now!'

There was a cry from the crowds, and some of the strongest animals were sent to see if the giraffe's story was true. As they went, Jeremy saw that they were still clutching the sticks they had used to beat his legs with.

One by one the little animals were helped from the burning schoolhouse and ran to their worried parents. What a noise! In the middle of it all, Otter's fire brigade arrived from another village. Everybody cheered as the red engine, bells clanging, rushed into the playground. The hoses were quickly reeled out and strong jets of water were aimed at the flames. The fire was soon put out.

Meanwhile, over at the Town Hall, Fox peeped in at the window. His eyes opened wide with shock! All the glass cases where the village silver should have been were empty! The tail of a weasel was just disappearing through a window.

'It *is* the weasels! They've robbed the Town Hall of its silver! Quick, round to the side. We might still catch them!'

The bushes at the side of the Town Hall were thick, and though the animals searched everywhere, the weasels could not be found.

The little group, with Fox in the lead, ran back to the schoolhouse and told the villagers what they had seen.

'What a day! This terrible fire, our children in danger, and now our Town Hall has been robbed,' cried a mother hedgehog.

Once he had seen that the children were all safe, Jeremy thought about the weasels again. He knew they would have to get back across the river to safety. He also knew that his long legs would take him to the river in a moment.

'Follow me!' he shouted.

Telling the villagers to hide in the bushes, Jeremy waded into the river and stood astride the log-crossing. There, head down, he waited. At last the weasels appeared, laughing as they ran. But their laughter stopped when they saw Jeremy.

Suddenly the villagers broke through the bushes and a struggle started. It wasn't long before the weasels were tied up and the sacks of silver were safe. The villagers cheered and cheered. At last they made their way back to the village to the children who had seen everything from the playground.

During all the noise and bustle, Jeremy went slowly and sadly back to his home. No one seemed to notice him go. Not one of the animals had spoken to him or thanked him. Still nobody wanted him, he thought.

In the playground the Mayor of Chestnut Village, Brock Badger, called for silence. Then he thanked the otters for their hard work in putting out the fire.

'It was very good of you,' he said, 'to come to the help of another village. The school is not badly damaged. I'm sure . . . '

Suddenly a small voice broke in. It was Jeremy's friend, the little mouse.

'What about the animal across the river?' she cried. '*He* saved us. The fire was burning our schoolroom and the otters would never have reached us in time. The animal came, even though we've all been horrible to him, and we never even said thank you.'

'Yes,' said the fox. 'And what about the silver? We've got that back, thanks to him.'

Then the little mouse burst into tears. Before long other animals started crying. At last the Mayor spoke.

'Folks of Chestnut Village!' he said, 'we have made a terrible mistake. We have hated another animal just because he didn't look like any of us. It has taken the smallest person in our village to show us how wrong we have been. This little mouse has helped us to see him for the good, brave animal he is. Let us all go and beg his forgiveness, if it's not too late. We might even be able to help *him*.'

A large tear was rolling down Jeremy's face as he sat alone, looking round his home. At least back at his old home he had friends. Perhaps he could put up with his owner's cruelty if he could be with his friends again.

At last he decided.

'I must go out of the wood and along by the fields. Once I reach the road I'll soon be caught and returned to the small field with the big fence.'

His eyes filled with tears again, but he slowly went out of his door and walked towards the fields.

'Stop!'

'Wait!'

'Please don't go!'

Voices rang out behind him, and Jeremy turned to see all the animals with their bright eyes and serious, sooty faces. The Mayor stepped forward. Silence fell.

Clearing his throat and looking up at Jeremy, the Mayor spoke:

'I hope you will excuse us running after you like this, but we had to come and speak to you before you left. We are *so* sorry for the way we treated you. We've all been wrong and unkind. I know I speak for everyone when I say I hope you will stay and become our friend.'

At this, Brock Badger looked around at the animals, who all nodded, smiling. It was quiet for a moment, then the little mouse spoke up.

'Please don't go! You're my special friend!'

Jeremy lowered his head, and she climbed quickly on and sat between his ears. Raising his head gently, so she wouldn't fall, Jeremy looked around and said, 'I'll stay.'

A loud cheer went up, and everyone crowded round Jeremy, shouting for joy. He suddenly felt all warm and happy. Then he heard his special friend laughing, and he could feel her jumping up and down on his head and waving her little white hanky.